EXPLORING WORLD CULTURES

Brazil

Alicia Z. Klepeis

Cavendish
Square

New York

Published in 2017 by Cavendish Square Publishing, LLC
243 5th Avenue, Suite 136, New York, NY 10016

Copyright © 2017 by Cavendish Square Publishing, LLC

First Edition

Library of Congress Cataloging-in-Publication Data

Names: Klepeis, Alicia, 1971- author.
Title: Brazil / Alicia Z. Klepeis.
Description: New York : Cavendish Square Publishing, [2016] | Series:
Exploring world cultures | Includes index.
Identifiers: LCCN 2016004973 (print) | LCCN 2016005568 (ebook) |
ISBN 9781502618108 (pbk.) | ISBN 9781502618023 (library bound) |
ISBN 9781502617880 (6 pack) | ISBN 9781502617385 (ebook)
Subjects: LCSH: Brazil--Juvenile literature.
Classification: LCC F2508.5 .K54 2016 (print) | LCC F2508.5 (ebook) |
DDC 981--dc23
LC record available at http://lccn.loc.gov/2016004973

Editorial Director: David McNamara
Editor: Kristen Susienka
Copy Editor: Rebecca Rohan
Art Director: Jeffrey Talbot
Designer: Joseph Macri
Production Assistant: Karol Szymczuk
Photo Research: J8 Media

Printed in the United States of America

Contents

Introduction

Brazil is a country in South America. It has many celebrations and traditions. Its history is rich. Brazil is home to more people than any other country in South America. It is a unique nation. Lots of different people live there. Many speak their own languages.

People have lived in Brazil for a long time. The Portuguese ruled Brazil for hundreds of years. Today, it is a free country. Brazil is South America's largest **democracy**. People have many kinds of jobs there. Some work in factories or mines. Others work in schools, hospitals, or hotels.

Brazil has many beautiful places. There are rain forests, swamps, rivers, and mountains. Many colorful plants and unusual animals live there. People also visit Brazil's lovely beaches.

Music and the arts are important to the Brazilian people. They celebrate different festivals throughout the year.

Brazil is an amazing country to explore.

Golden lion tamarins are native to Brazil's Atlantic coastal forest. They are an endangered species.

Brazil is in South America. It is the fifth-biggest country on Earth. It is a little smaller than the United States and covers over 3 million square miles (8.52 million square kilometers).

The Amazon River is in Brazil. It is the world's longest river. The Atlantic Ocean borders Brazil's east coast. Brazil touches every country in South America except Ecuador and Chile.

This map of Brazil shows the country's many rivers. Red dots mark the nation's cities.

Most of Brazil has warm weather. Some places have rainfall throughout the year. Other areas have a dry season.

Brazil is mostly flat. There are grassy areas called *pampas* in the south. The Brazilian Highlands have low mountains and river valleys.

The Amazon rain forest is in Brazil. It is the world's biggest rain forest. It has millions of different bugs. Many plants and animals live there, too. Fruits like mangoes, guavas, and cashew apples grow there.

FACT!

The Amazon River is home to a pink dolphin called the *boto*.

A pink river dolphin

History

People have lived in Brazil for thousands of years. The earliest people hunted animals, gathered wild plants, and fished. Later, they farmed.

This illustration shows how sugarcane was processed in a Brazilian factory around 1700.

The first Europeans visited Brazil in 1500. Many Native people lived there. Portugal started to rule Brazil in the 1500s. Portuguese settlers forced the Native people to work on their **plantations**. They also brought in slaves from Africa.

Brazil gained independence in 1822. During the 1800s, schools, libraries, roads, and railways were built. In 1889, Brazil became a **republic** with a president.

The military took over Brazil's government from 1964 to 1985. Since 1985, Brazilians have voted for their leaders. They are working to improve their country so all people have a brighter future.

FACT!

After slavery ended in 1888, many people around the world came to work in Brazil.

The Father of the Poor

Getúlio Vargas was elected president of Brazil in 1930. He helped improve working and living conditions for many Brazilians.

Getúlio Vargas

Brazil is the largest democracy in South America. It has twenty-six states and one federal district. Brasilia is Brazil's capital.

Brazil's government has three parts:

1) Legislative: This part of the government is called the National Congress. People in the National Congress write new laws.

2) Judicial: The courts make up this part of Brazil's government. They follow the country's constitution. The constitution was signed in 1988. It describes all the basic laws of Brazil.

First Female Leader

Dilma Rousseff became Brazil's first female president in 2011.

President Rousseff

3) Executive: The president, the vice president, and the **cabinet** ministers make up this part of the government. They make sure laws are obeyed.

Brazil's National Congress has two parts. The Senate has 81 members. The Chamber of Deputies has 513 members. They gather in the National Congress building in Brasilia to pass laws.

FACT!

All Brazilian citizens between eighteen and seventy years old must vote in elections.

The Economy

Brazil has the largest **economy** in Latin America. It sells and buys goods from countries around the world. Brazilian workers make many kinds of goods.

A worker paints a car in the assembly line at a Nissan factory in Resende, Brazil.

In Brazil's cities, factory workers make lots of different products. They build computers, cars, and airplanes. They make shoes and clothing. They also produce cement, lumber, and steel. Many city workers have service jobs. Some work as tour guides or shopkeepers. Others are teachers or lawyers.

Brazil produces many gemstones. These are often made into beautiful pieces of jewelry.

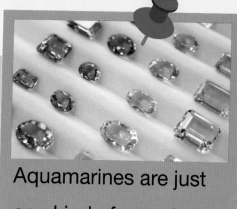

Aquamarines are just one kind of gemstones found in Brazil.

In the countryside, many Brazilians are farmers. They grow crops such as sugarcane, cocoa, coffee, and oranges. Brazil is also an important meat producer.

Mining is another big industry in Brazil. Minerals found here include bauxite, copper, and gold. Iron ore is Brazil's biggest **export** today.

Dams

Waterpower is a very important source of energy in Brazil. Many dams have been built in the Amazon River basin.

The Environment

The people, animals, and plants of Brazil need clean water and clean air to live. Not everywhere in the country has these things. Brazil's large cities are overcrowded. Many people live in poor areas called *favelas*.

This is a poor neighborhood in Rio de Janeiro.

Many favelas don't have garbage pickup. Pollution from cars and businesses makes the air dirty.

Brazil is home to different plants and animals. Many live in the Amazon rain forest. Unfortunately, people are cutting down the rain forest to build farms and roads, and to mine. Many plants and animals are in danger of becoming extinct.

The Brazilian people and government are working to make their country cleaner.

Recycling is just starting in some parts of Brazil. Several plants recycle aluminum cans. They turn them into new sheets of metal.

Aluminum cans are gathered at a collection center in Brazil.

Droughts

For decades, Brazil has struggled with droughts (dry spells). This is tough for farmers growing crops and for city dwellers.

Over 200 million people live in Brazil. It is the most populated country in South America.

A group of young girls have fun at the Sao Martin street children's center in Rio.

There are about 240 tribes of Native people in Brazil. They make up less than 0.5 percent of Brazil's population. The Guarani people are the largest group. They live mainly in the southwest. The Tikuna is the biggest tribe in the Amazon. Many tribes have their own special traditions.

Over its history, people from around the world have settled in Brazil. Immigrants have come

Japanese in Brazil

The city of São Paulo has the biggest Japanese community in the world outside of Japan.

from Italy, Germany, Japan, and other countries. Brazilians of different backgrounds have married and had children. Today, many Brazilians have a mixed heritage. Just over half of the population described themselves as black or mixed race in the 2010 Brazilian census.

FACT!

Nearly one-quarter of Brazil's population is under fifteen years old.

Lifestyle

Brazilian people have different ways of living. People in the city live differently than people in the countryside.

Many high-rise buildings make up the landscape of Rio de Janeiro.

City families might live in a tall apartment or a house made of scrap materials. They might ride the subway or drive to work. Families in the city might have cell phones, computers, and cars.

People living in the country often farm and raise animals for food. Others work in mines. Many country homes don't have running water or electricity.

FACT!

Over 85 percent of Brazilians live in cities and towns.

Women used to stay home to take care of their children and their homes. Today, women's roles are changing. The same number of girls and boys attend elementary school. More women go to college. They might work as businesspeople, lawyers, or doctors.

Houses in the Amazon

Families along the Amazon River may live in houses on stilts.

Religion

Religion is important to many people in Brazil. Today, about 65 percent of Brazilians are Roman Catholic. Brazil has more Roman Catholics than any other country in the world.

Candomblé followers carry flower baskets onto a boat in a ceremony honoring Yemenjá, goddess of the sea.

FACT!

Brazil has no official religion. People are free to believe what they want.

The number of Protestants in Brazil is growing. So is the number of Brazilians who do not practice any religion at all. Both Protestants and Catholics are Christian. They celebrate

Christmas and Easter. Their church services often include music.

In addition to Christianity, some Brazilians follow other religions. Candomblé is a religion that combines

The Cathedral of Brasilia

religious traditions brought to Brazil by African slaves with those of Catholicism. Candomblé followers worship an all-powerful god named Oludumaré as well as other gods.

The Pope

In 2013, Pope Francis visited Brazil. Over three million people attended a Mass held on Copacabana Beach.

Language

More than two hundred languages are spoken in Brazil. The most common language is Portuguese. Almost everyone in Brazil speaks Portuguese. Brazil is the only

A bilingual sign in Recife

country in Latin America to have Portuguese as its main language.

FACT!

Bom dia (boom dee-ah) means "hello" in Portuguese.

Portuguese is also Brazil's official language. It is used by the Brazilian government, in schools, and for business matters.

Many of Brazil's Native groups speak their own languages. Tupí, Arawak, Carib, and Gê are some of the main language groups spoken in Brazil. Unfortunately, many of these languages are in danger of dying out.

Lots of people in Brazil learn to speak more than one language. Kids often learn English or Spanish at school. Immigrants have also brought German, Italian, and Japanese to Brazil.

Other Languages

Besides Portuguese, some Brazilian states have additional official languages. For example, Talian is a co-official language in Rio Grande do Sul and Santa Catarina states.

Brazilians enjoy arts of all kinds. Music is a huge part of their culture. Jazzy bossa nova music was invented by João Gilberto in Rio de Janeiro in the 1950s. Brazilian musicians also create their own pop and rock music today.

A Baiana woman celebrates Independence Day.

In addition to music, Brazilians love dance. Samba is a popular dance. Samba has its roots in African dance and music rhythms.

Most people in Brazil have TVs. Soap operas are popular programs. Soccer matches also attract lots of viewers.

Spaceship Museum

Brazilians enjoy visiting museums. The Modern Art Museum in Rio de Janeiro looks like a spaceship!

Brazilians enjoy many festivals. The biggest, Carnival, usually takes place in February. Brazilians also celebrate many religious and national holidays.

Brazil's Independence Day is on September 7. Marching bands play. Fireworks and parades mark the occasion across the country.

FACT!

Cândido Portinari is one of Brazil's most famous painters. His works often show the lives of peasant workers.

Fun and Play

There are lots of ways to have fun in Brazil.

Soccer is the most popular sport. Brazil hosted the World Cup in 2014. Volleyball is another sport Brazilians love to play. It is the most-practiced sport by young girls. People often play it on the beach. Capoeira is a unique activity that combines movements from dance and fighting. African slaves in Brazil helped develop it.

People play music and practice capoeira on a beach in Rio de Janeiro.

FACT!

São Paulo's Ibirapuera Park has biking trails, playgrounds, an art museum, and lots more!

Soccer Success

Brazil's national soccer team has won the World Cup five times. That's more than any other country!

The Brazilian national soccer team in 2014.

Brazilian people enjoy games. One traditional game is called Queimada. It is a kind of tag with two teams of players. There is no limit to how many people can play at one time. Other popular games include checkers, jump rope, and card games.

Food

Feijoada

Brazilians eat lots of different foods. In northeastern Brazil, people often eat African-style foods. These foods include nuts, fish, and coconut. Brazilians who live in the south often eat lots of beef. People commonly eat fish along the coast and the Amazon River.

Feijoada is Brazil's national dish. It is popular all over Brazil. This stew is made of smoked pork and beef, rice, and black beans. It is usually served with greens and orange slices.

There are about 12,500 restaurants just in the city of São Paulo alone!

Brazilians eat lots of fruit. Oranges, mangoes, and pineapple grow here. But Brazil also has more unusual fruits. These include açaí (a small dark berry), guava, and passion fruit.

People in Brazil often drink coffee, a tea called *maté*, fruit juice, soft drinks, and bottled water.

Chocolate Delight

A *brigadeiro* is a small chocolate treat. Brigadeiros are often served at parties.

Brigadeiros

29

Glossary

cabinet   A group of advisors that helps the leader of a government.

democracy   A system of government in which leaders are chosen by the people.

economy   A system made up of a country's imports, exports, and successful industries.

export   An item a country makes but sells and sends to another country.

plantation   An agricultural estate worked by laborers; crops are grown here, especially to be sold.

republic   A government that has a leader who is not a king or queen and is usually a president.

Find Out More

Books

Richardson, Margaret. *Brazil*. Letters From
Around the World. Twickenham, UK:
Cherrytree Books, 2016.

Savery, Annabel. *Brazil.* Been There! Mankato, MN:
Smart Apple Media, 2012.

Website

A Day in the Life: Brazil

www.timeforkids.com/destination/brazil/day-in-life

Video

Brazil: Supplying the Amazon

videos.howstuffworks.com/discovery/7246-
brazil-supplying-the-amazon-video.htm#.
Vqd0h0ZAkwM.mailto

This video shows how goods get to the most
remote communities along the Amazon River.

Index

About the Author

Alicia Z. Klepeis began her career at the National Geographic Society. She is the author of many kids' books, including *The World's Strangest Foods*, *Bizarre Things We've Called Medicine*, *Francisco's Kites*, and *From Pizza to Pisa*. She lives with her family in upstate New York.